Spies and Spying

HOW SPIES WORK

K.C. Kelley

FRANKLIN WATTS
LONDON·SYDNEY

An Appleseed Editions book

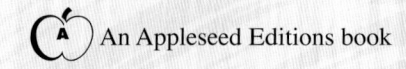

First published in 2009 by Franklin Watts

Franklin Watts
338 Euston Road, London NW1 3BH

Franklin Watts Australia
Level 17/207 Kent St, Sydney, NSW 2000

© 2009 Appleseed Editions

Appleseed Editions Ltd
Well House, Friars Hill, Guestling, East Sussex TN35 4ET

Created by Q2AMedia
Editor: Honor Head
Art Director: Rahul Dhiman
Designer: Ranjan Singh
Picture Researcher: Shreya Sharma
Line Artist: Sibi N. Devasia
Colouring Artist: Mahender Kumar

All rights reserved. No part of this publication may be reproduced, stored in a retrieval system or transmitted in any form or by any means, electronic, mechanical, photocopying, recording or otherwise, without prior permission of the publisher.

ISBN 978 0 7496 8795 3

Dewey classification: 327.12

All words in **bold** can be found in Glossary on pages 30–31.

Website information is correct at time of going to press. However, the publishers cannot accept liability for any information or links found on third-party websites.

A CIP catalogue for this book is available from the British Library.

Picture credits
t=top b=bottom c=centre l=left r=right

Cover: Michael Crockett Photography/ Photolibrary, Inset Image: Q2AMedia: t, Q2AMedia: c, Marjan Laznik/ iStockphoto: b.

Insides: Marjan Laznik/ iStockphoto: Title Page, Andrew Howe/ iStockphoto: 4l, Peter Hince/ Stone/Getty Images: 5t, Michael Ledray/ Shutterstock: 5b, Jamie McDonald/ Getty Images: 6r, Marjan Laznik/ iStockphoto: 7b, Gramper/ Bigstockphoto: 8r, Olivier Le Queinec/ Dreamstime: 8b, Mark Stout/ Dreamstime: 9r, Michael Crockett Photography/ Photolibrary: 10b, Ursula/ Shutterstock: 11t, SSG Bronco Suzuki/ Defence Imagery.Mil: 11b, Mark Finkenstaedt: 12r, Shutterstock: 13b, Ed Holub/ Photolibrary: 14b, Lars Topelmann/ Photolibrary: 15b, Rob Lang/ Photolibrary: 16l, Dennis Cook/ Associated Press: 17l, FBI/ U.S. Federal Government/ U.S. Department of Justice.: 17b, Clarence S Lewis/ Shutterstock: 18b, National Security Agency/ Central Security Service: 19t, Evening Standard/ Hulton Archive/ Getty Images: 19b, National Archives: 20t, National Archives: 21l, Dhoxax/ Shutterstock: 23t, Norman Chan/ Shutterstock: 23b, STR/ Associated Press: 24r, Dave Bartruff/ Corbis: 25t, Owen Price/ iStockphoto: 27b, Krzysztof Zmij/ iStockphoto: 28r, C. Benton: 28b, NASA Images: 29b, Andrew Howe/ iStockphoto: 31.
Q2A Media Art Bank: 7, 9, 13, 17, 20, 22, 25, 26.

Printed in China

Franklin Watts is a division of Hachette Children's Books,
an Hachette Livre UK company.
www.hachettelivre.co.uk

CONTENTS

Spies at work 4

Spy skills 6

In the shadows 8

Stealing secrets 10

Those who know 14

Sending secrets home 18

Tricks of the trade 22

Fighting back 26

High-tech spying 28

Glossary 30

Index and Webfinder 32

SPIES AT WORK

For centuries, rulers and governments have had secrets that other people want to know about. This is why nearly every country has spies – to find out things people don't want found out!

Working in secret

Governments have many secrets, such as plans for war, deadly weapons or just important information. Enemies of those governments want to uncover those secrets. To do this they turn to the silent experts – spies. A spy usually works for one side against another, finding hidden information. Being a spy can be an exciting but it can also be dangerous.

Spies use lots of everyday equipment to find secrets.

Spies and Spying

Spies must learn to follow people without being noticed to find out information.

The quiet service

Spies have many skills. They have to learn where secret information is kept and how to find that information. Spies have to be a combination of burglars, con artists, technical wizards, language experts and even great shots.

SPY FILE

Nathan Hale

One of America's first spies was Nathan Hale. He was sent to spy on the British in New York during the **American War of Independence.** Hale was captured and hanged by the British in 1776. Before he died he said: "I regret that I have only one life to give for my country."

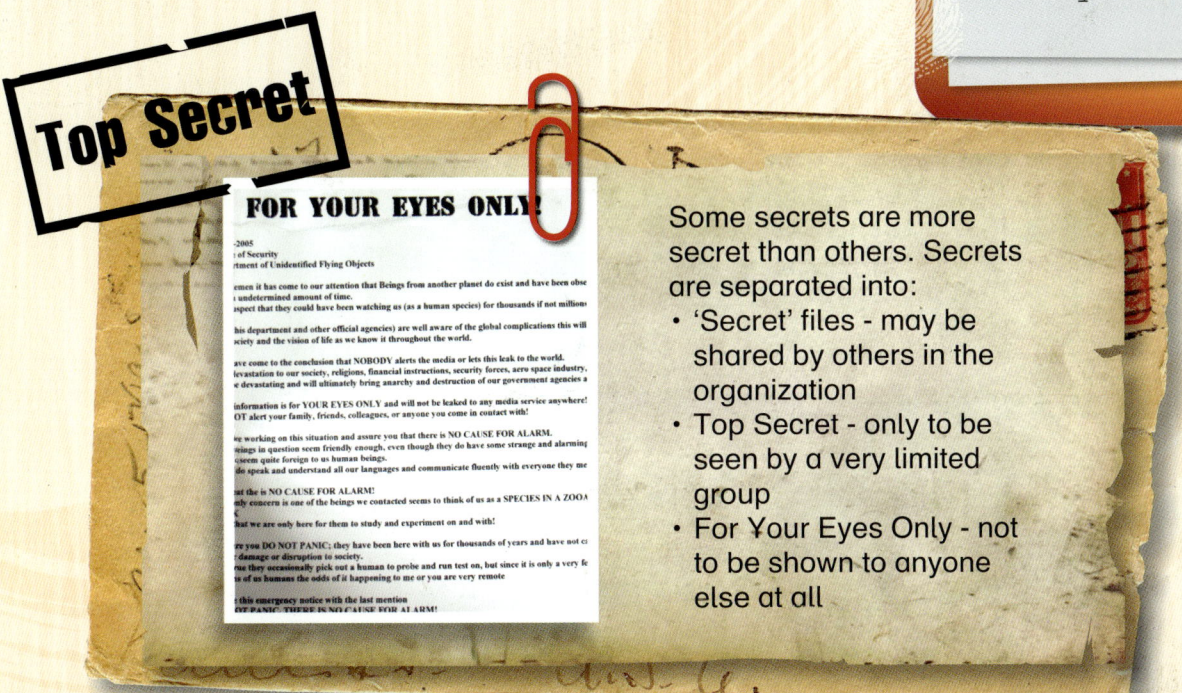

Top Secret

Some secrets are more secret than others. Secrets are separated into:
- 'Secret' files - may be shared by others in the organization
- Top Secret - only to be seen by a very limited group
- For Your Eyes Only - not to be shown to anyone else at all

SPY SKILLS

How do you become a spy? Like any tough job, there's a lot to learn first! Training is hard and you need to build up lots of skills, from acting to shooting!

Getting fit

Spies have to be physically fit. At places like the **CIA** in the USA, where they train spies, they have a tough training programme. Trainee spies practise using weapons and learn face-to-face fighting. Spies often have to pretend to be someone else, so they must learn how to make different facial expressions and body movements. Learning how to act is an important part of their training.

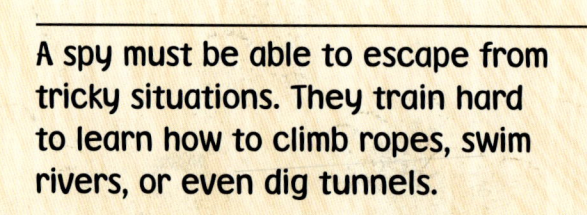

A spy must be able to escape from tricky situations. They train hard to learn how to climb ropes, swim rivers, or even dig tunnels.

Spies and Spying

Getting brainy

Spies spend more time in classrooms than they do in the gym. They learn languages they might need to speak if they are going to a foreign country, and tricks such as how to disguise themselves. They practise making and breaking codes and they work with experts in radio and other technology that will help them **intercept** secrets. If they are going to be sent to a new country, they carefully study maps and other information about their destination.

SPY FILE

Stella Rimington

Many women have been top spies or have worked in the secret services. In 1992, Stella Rimington was the first woman to lead a national spy agency. She ran Britain's MI5 organisation. She now writes best-selling detective thrillers.

Top Secret

Both sides in any war know that the other side is using spies. If one side captures an enemy spy, they sometimes use the spy to bargain. They might agree to swap the captured spy in exchange for information or for one of their own captured spies.

Learning to use firearms is an important skill for many spies. But guns are only used when absolutely necessary.

7

IN THE SHADOWS

Once the training is over, a spy has to go out into the field to uncover the secret information that is needed. But those secrets are usually well hidden ...

Finding secrets

The first step for a spy is to find out where the secrets or information are hidden. To do this, the spy may try to win the trust and friendship of his enemies so that they reveal information by mistake. But this could take a long time. It might be quicker for a spy to search the building where the secrets are held. For instance, there is a good chance that the plans for a new rocket could be in a government science building.

Where are secrets kept? Often behind locked doors. Spies carry special tools like these 'lock picks' to break open doors and locks.

Picking a lock means opening it without using the key. With most locks, it is easy for a trained spy. New electronic locks, however, are harder to open. Now spies have to use special electronic cards that can read the locks' combinations.

Spies and Spying

Breaking in

When they know where the secrets are kept, spies have to wait for darkness, or for a time when the building is empty, to search it. To reach their target building, spies might have to talk their way past a guard, put on a disguise or pretend to be someone who works there. Or they might have to pick a lock, scale a wall or break a window. They do whatever it takes to get inside safely and quietly.

Breaking into buildings quickly and quietly is a special spy skill.

SPY FILE

Jonathan Pollard

In 1985, an employee of the US navy named Jonathan Pollard was caught with a briefcase that held 60 **classified** documents. Many were stamped 'Top Secret'. It was discovered that Jonathan had been smuggling out and selling military secrets to Israeli agents and others for more than a year.

Hidden bugs

If you can't take a picture of a secret, you might be able to hear it. Spies used to hide inside rooms and hope to overhear something. But now spies can hide **microphones** or **bugs** in just about anything. Bugs are used to record conversations and are tiny enough to be hidden in a plug socket, a calculator or under a phone. The Soviet Union once sent a carving to hang on the wall of the US Embassy in Moscow. Inside the carving was a hidden microphone!

Top Secret

If you can't plant a bug in an office, you might still be able to listen in. Special devices shoot laser beams at windows. The windows vibrate when there is noise or talking inside the room. The laser 'reads' the vibrations and translates them into sound . . . which you can hear. Clever!

Powerful microphones can be concealed just about anywhere. This mike was placed inside a fake tree stump to record a conversation outdoors.

Spies and Spying

Phone taps

People do a lot of talking on the telephone, so '**tapping**' into those conversations can reveal many secrets. Spies plant bugs in phones, phone lines and phone poles. These bugs either tape the conversation or send them to another phone where the spy can listen in. Calls from mobile phones can be intercepted, too. Also, as more and more people use computers to make calls, spies are starting to listen in using special software bugs.

SPY FILE

Bugged!

In the late 1940s the FBI wanted to prove that Judy Conlon was a Soviet spy. To do this, FBI agents planted bugs in her home and office. By listening to her plot with other agents, they gathered enough evidence to arrest and convict her.

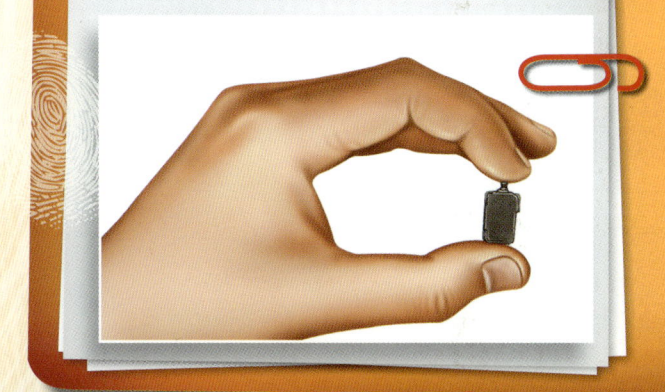

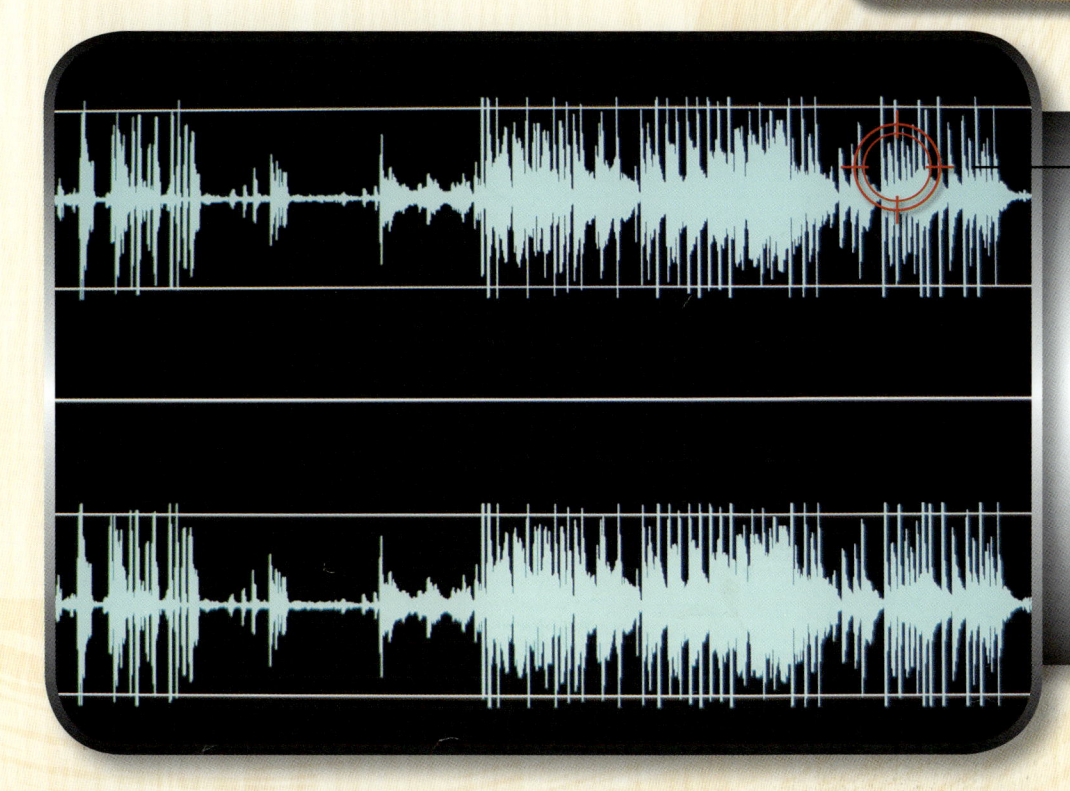

Sounds recorded by hidden microphones can be read as sound waves like the ones shown here. These sound waves can also be analysed by electronic machines to make them clearer.

13

Those Who Know

Sometimes the information needed is more difficult to find. To get these secrets, spies have to be more creative ... and some have to go under cover.

Secrets for money

One of the best ways to get secret information is simply to buy it. People who know secrets will sometimes pass that information to a spy for cash. The person who provides the secrets won't give the spy away, either. If they did, they would be in serious trouble with the people they had stolen the secrets from.

Some people have made a lot of money by selling secrets for cash.

Blackmail!

Not all people will be tempted by money. Sometimes they have to be forced to tell their secrets. Threatening to reveal a personal secret about someone – such as a crime in their past – is called blackmail. It can be used to make someone give you what you want – but first you have to find something to blackmail them with.

> Spies will use threats or blackmail to force people to give them secret information.

SPY FILE

Under cover

In the early 1980s, a team of Israeli spies set up a business in Khartoum, Sudan, pretending to be travel resort owners. But they were really bribing government officials to let them smuggle Jewish people out of Ethiopia. The Jewish people were being oppressed by their government so the Israeli spies used money and a clever plan to save them.

SENDING SECRETS HOME

Once they've got the secrets, spies have to get them to their bosses safely. Spies have to be just as careful sending information as finding it.

Using codes

One way to send information that no one else can read is to put it in code. But it has to be done in a way that the person receiving it can decode the message. Learning how to code and decode messages is a big part of the work of a spy. Codes might be simply switching letters around, or the use of symbols instead of letters. Other codes might use a 'key' that has been carefully thought out by the intelligence agency.

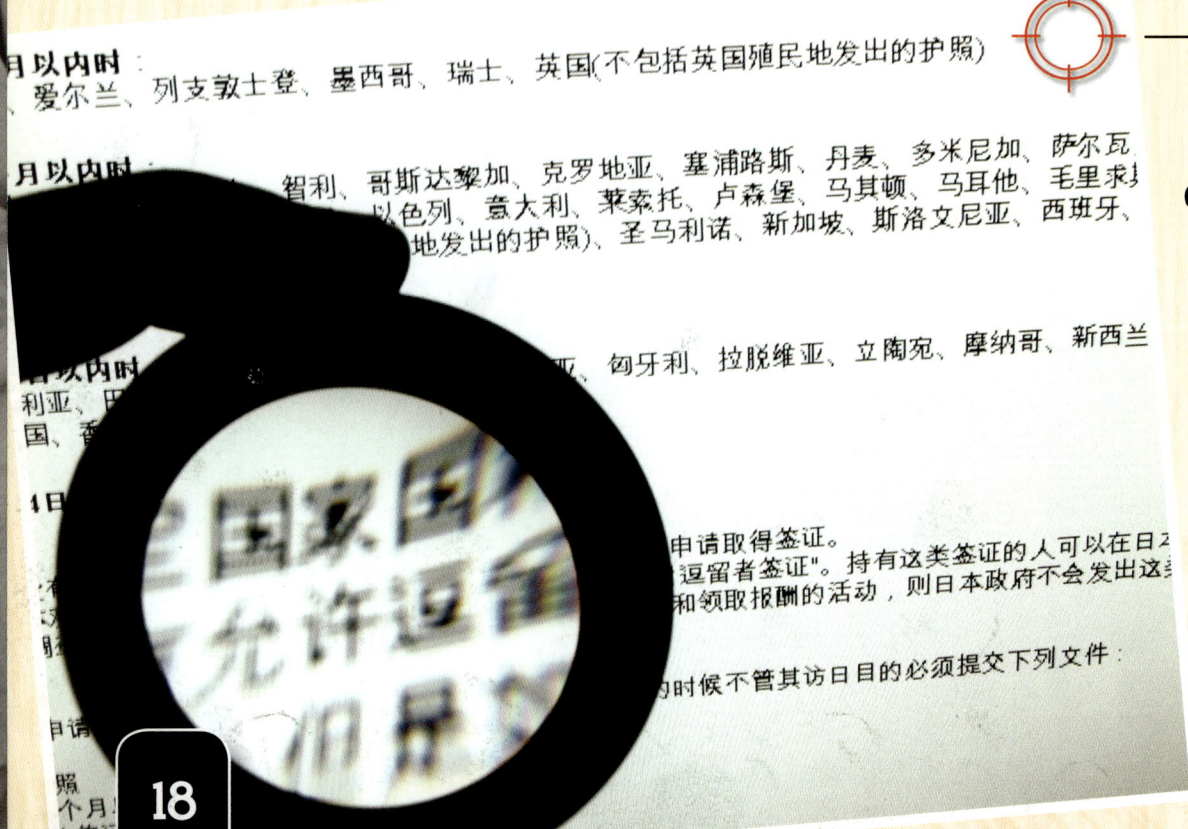

Codes can be written in any language. This Chinese text might have characters switched around to give a spy a secret message.

Spies and Spying

Top Secret

Early in World War II, British military leaders knew that if they could crack the German code, they could gain a huge advantage. Using a captured German Enigma code machine, a team of some of the greatest minds in England gathered at a mansion in Bletchley Park, outside London. For nearly the entire war they worked in complete secrecy. They decoded German information and saved thousands of lives.

Breaking a code

Intelligence agencies use experts in **cryptography** to study and break enemy codes. Today, code breakers have computers to help them to decode enemy messages.

In this building and others at Bletchley Park in England, code breakers helped the **Allies** win World War II.

Using radios

During World War II, the US Army used native Navajo speakers to pass messages that the enemy could not translate.

Ever since radio was invented, spies have been using it to stay in touch with their bosses. Often they would transmit at an agreed time. The spy might just say his or her message or use **Morse code** to tap out the message, which would then be decoded at the other end.

Top Secret

Robert Baden Powell (1857-1941), who founded the Scout Movement, pretended to study butterflies on spying trips abroad. He'd sketch a butterfly, which was really a plan of an enemy building. This butterfly shows the plan of an enemy **fortress** - the patch in the middle is the layout while the markings show the size and position of the guns.

20

Spies and Spying

Hidden radios

Before mobile phones, a spy's radio was his most important tool. Radios could be hidden in many ways, such as behind cabinets, under floors, or inside small briefcases. The **antennas** for these radios might have been disguised as TV aerials, stereo speaker wires, or even washing lines. Spies were taught how to work the radios and how to fix them if they broke.

SPY FILE

Morse code

In the 1830s, Samuel F.B. Morse created a way for people to send messages by telegraph. The telegraph sent electrical signals along a wire. Morse thought of a way to make those signals into words. In his code, a person taps in dots or dashes that represent different letters of the alphabet. A machine at the other end taps out the same code, which is then 'read' by someone listening. Morse code is still used today.

Radios and transmitters can be hidden in many places. An enemy searching a spy might not think to look in the heel of his shoe for this transmitter.

TRICKS OF THE TRADE

If you are constantly being watched and followed, passing on secrets can be a problem. However, there are a few tricks every spy knows ...

Dead drops

The most common way to pass messages between spies and their **controllers** is the **dead drop**. For instance, a dead drop might be under a park bench. The spy will let the controller know when and where the package will be. The spy then leaves it there. Later, the controller will collect the package. This way the spy and the controller never meet.

A chalk mark on a tree shows where a dead drop might be placed.

Spies and Spying

Passing in public

Sometimes there's no time to arrange a dead drop, so spies have to 'pass' secrets. This means that the spy and the controller meet in public but do not to speak or even seem to know each other. They pass very close to one another, on a busy street, for example. The spy slips the message to the controller without anyone seeing. This might be done by putting the message into a pocket or shopping bag.

> Expert passing is done so well that anyone watching will not see that something has been passed.

Top Secret

One way that spies used to pass messages was through the newspaper. They would place a small ad in the paper, using everyday language but containing a code word. A fellow spy would read the ad, see the code word, and know that something was waiting for him at their dead drop.

Disguises

Another way that a spy might stay out of sight is by staying in disguise. Some spies use fake beards and moustaches, colour their hair, wear coloured contact lenses and other disguise aids to make them look completely different. They might use a cane or even wear a fake plaster to pretend they have a broken leg or arm. One male spy in France in the 1750s pretended to be a woman for more than 30 years in order to spy on the British!

Top Secret

In 1980, Antonio Mendez, head of disguise at the CIA, helped six people disguise themselves so that they could leave an embassy in Iran where they were being held **hostage**.

These photos show the many different looks of German spy Dieter Kunzelmann.

Spies and Spying

A false wall might hide a spy during a search. This picture shows panels removed to reveal a secret place inside the walls.

Hiding places

Sometimes a spy has to hide out. Many spies living in an enemy country build false rooms into their homes or have a small chamber hidden under the floorboards. Other spies have used trunks or barrels to 'post' themselves home after their spy missions were over. Mary Queen of Scots (1542-1587) used spies in barrels to help plan her escapes. German agents during World War II parachuted into England inside barrel-shaped containers.

SPY FILE

Antonio Mendez

Antonio Mendez was a master at making people look like someone else. For more than 30 years he made sure that CIA agents could hide almost anywhere. Today, Mendez gives lectures and writes books on his adventures.

FIGHTING BACK

Being caught is almost worse than being killed. A spy caught by the enemy might be forced to work for them and betray his own country.

Secret weapons

A spy hopes never to have to use a weapon but has to be ready to defend himself if trapped by the enemy. Weapons have to be carefully and cunningly disguised. Guns can be hidden inside lipstick tubes, walking sticks, belts, pens or inside shoes in hollow heels. A wire attached to a wristwatch can be used to choke a guard.

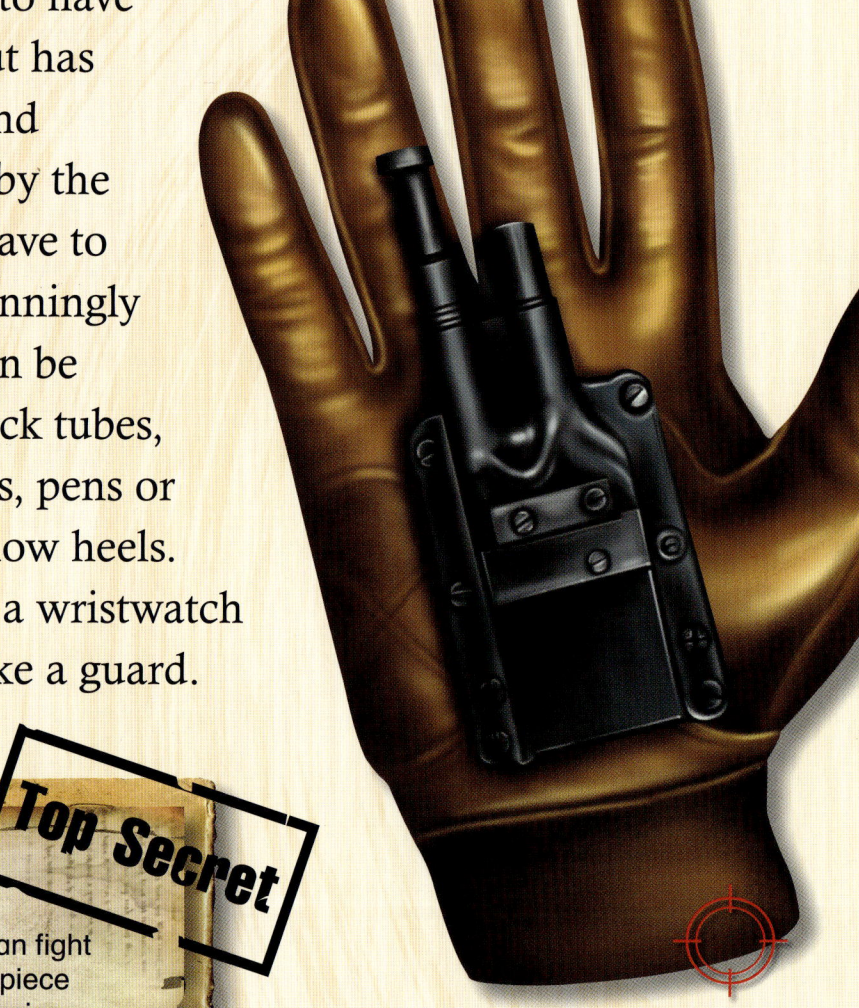

Top Secret

One way that a spy can fight back is with a simple piece of jewellery - the killer ring. This ring is pretty from one side only. The inside edge is as sharp as a knife and can be used to slash an attacker.

This tiny gun could be hidden inside a glove.

Spies and Spying

Ka-boom!

Sometimes the worst way to hurt your enemy is not to steal their secrets . . . but to just blow the secrets up! Spies who destroy information are called **saboteurs**. They might sneak in to a military post at night and plant a time bomb that will go off hours later. Learning how to make and conceal explosives is part of a spy's training. They can take household chemicals and an alarm clock and make a lot of trouble behind enemy lines.

SPY FILE

Getting Castro

In the early 1960s, US spies tried to kill the then Cuban leader Fidel Castro several times. They tried poisoning him and sending assassins after him. It is claimed they used a case of poisoned wine and exploding cigars in attempts to kill him.

Spies usually do not try to blow up people, just places. They might use special materials, such as wire and plastic explosive, to make a time bomb.

27

HIGH-TECH SPYING

Today's spies have a huge range of electronic and technical equipment they can use to make spying more efficient and safer.

Hacker spies

The use of computers has made spying a bit safer. Spies can 'hack' into the computer networks of their enemies to find secrets. They use software that helps them disable passwords. They might also write a program that disguises their true identity and allows them to pretend to be a part of the enemy's network. Today computer security against government or industrial spies is big business.

Huge amounts of information can be stored on tiny computer chips. So instead of snapping pictures of secret papers, today's spies steal these chips.

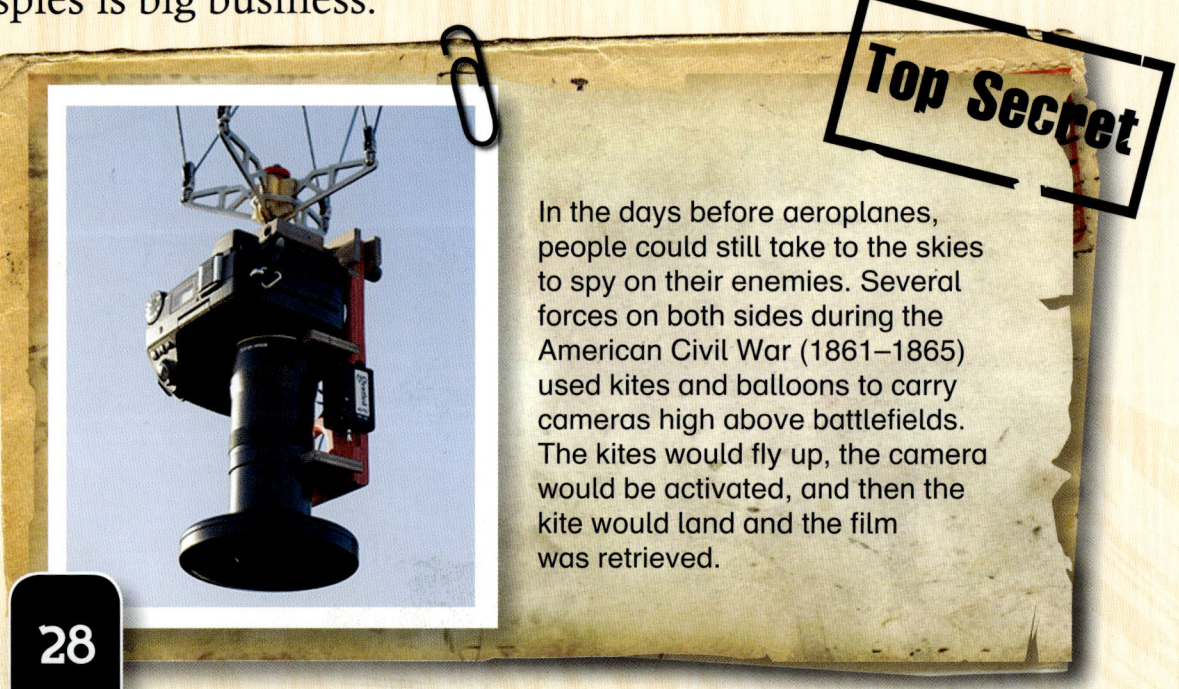

Top Secret

In the days before aeroplanes, people could still take to the skies to spy on their enemies. Several forces on both sides during the American Civil War (1861–1865) used kites and balloons to carry cameras high above battlefields. The kites would fly up, the camera would be activated, and then the kite would land and the film was retrieved.

Spies and Spying

Satellite spying

Another way of safe spying is through the use of satellites. From space they orbit the Earth and aim super-cameras at military bases in enemy countries. The satellites might track shipments of valuable cargo at sea or follow the enemy's troop movements.

Photos like this one of land in Egypt are taken by satellites. Spies can examine the photos to learn more about life in their enemy's country.

SPY FILE

Anti-terrorism

Many spies today fight terrorism and illegal activities. In 1992, police used spies to capture Abimael Guzman. His group, called Shining Path, killed more than 25,000 people in Peru over 20 years. Police planted a mole in his group who collected intelligence and worked in disguise as part of their plan to bring him to justice.

— land
— sea
— forest

GLOSSARY

American War of Independence   fought from 1775 to 1781, this war separated the American colonies (later the United States of America) from Great Britain

Allies   the countries that fought on the same side as Britain during World War II. The countries included France, Australia, USA and Russia

antennas   wires that receive radio signals from the air

blackmail   when a person is forced to give up information or money to prevent personal information from being revealed

bugs   Small electronic devices used to record sound

CIA   the Central Intelligence Agency, the main American spy agency operating outside the USA

classified   secrets that only certain people are allowed to see

controllers   people who organise and run the work of spies

cryptography   the science of making and breaking codes

dead drop   a public place where spies can drop messages and parcels for each other

fortress   a building that is used to protect soldiers or fighting equipment

hostage   a person who is held as a prisoner, to be exchanged for something from the enemy

Spies and Spying

intercept see or overhear a message or transmission meant for another person

KGB the Russian intelligence and security organisation

MI6 the UK's intelligence agency now called SIS (Secret Intelligence Service)

microphones devices that pick up, record and amplify sound

mole a spy who works inside the enemy's spy agency

Morse code an alphabet code made up of combinations of long and short sound signals

saboteurs people who deliberately destroy or damage enemy buildings or equipment

tapping secretly listening in to someone else's conversation, usually with an electronic bug or device

INDEX

agents   9, 13, 16, 25

blackmail   11, 15

cameras   10, 11, 28, 29
CIA   6, 17, 24, 15
codes   7, 18, 19, 20, 21, 23
controllers   22
cryptography   19

dead drop   22, 23

disguise   7, 9, 24, 29
double agents   16

firearms   7

hacker   28

intelligence agencies   16, 17, 19

lock picks   8

MI5   7

MI6   17
microphone   12, 13
moles   16, 17, 29
Morse code   20, 21

phone tapping   13

radios   7, 20, 21

saboteurs   27
satellite   29

undercover 14

WEBFINDER

www.spymuseum.org
Hundreds of pages of spy stuff, from secret equipment to spy stories and tales of famous spies

www.britishcouncil.org/kids-topics-spies.htm
This site has dozens of activities you can do to learn more about being a spy

www.idahoptv.org/dialogue4kids/season4/spy/
Learn more about the secret language of spies